In The Wild

Claire Robinson

Heinemann Library
Des Plaines, Illinois

Designed by Celia Floyd
Illustrations by Alan Fraser (Pennant Illustration)
Printed and bound in Hong Kong/China by South China Printing Co.

03 02 01 00 99
10 9 8 7 6 5 4 3 2 1

Library of Congress Cataloging-in-Publication Data

Robinson, Claire, 1955-
    Snakes / Claire Robinson.
       p. cm. – (In the wild)
    Includes bibliographical references (p.) and index.
    Summary: Introduces the physical characteristics, habitat, behavior, and life cycle of snakes, with an emphasis on the rattlesnake.
    ISBN 1-57572-864-8 (alk. Paper)
    1. Snakes—Juvenile literature. [1. Snakes. 2. Rattlesnakes.]
  I. Title. II. Series: Robinson, Claire, 1955- In the wild.
  QL666.O6R4835 1999
  597.96—dc21

                                     98-34029
                                     CIP
                                     AC

Acknowledgments
The Publishers would like to thank the following for permission to reproduce photographs:
Ardea London Ltd./P. Morris, p. 6; Bruce Coleman Limited/Charlie Ott, pp. 8, 9; John Cancalosi, pp. 13, 15; BBC Natural History Unit/John Cancalosi, pp. 7, 9; Jeff Foott, p. 21; London Zoo, p. 5 (left); NHPA/Stephen Dalton, p. 14; Oxford Scientific Films/Babs and Bert Wells, p. 4 (left); Animals Animals, pp. 11, 17; Zigmund Leszcynski, pp. 12, 16; Marty Cordano, p. 18; Jack Dermid, p. 19; John Cancalosi, p. 20; J.A.L. Cooke, p. 22; Wendy Shattil and Bob Rozinski, p. 23; Photo Researchers, Inc./G.C. Kelley, p. 5 (right); C.K. Lorenz, p. 10; Zoological Society of London, p. 4 (right).

Cover photograph: Photo Researchers Inc/G.C. Kelley.

Every effort has been made to contact copyright holders of any material reproduced in this book. Any omissions will be rectified in subsequent printings if notice is given to the Publisher.

Some words are shown in bold, **like this**. You can find out what they mean by looking in the glossary.

Contents

Snake Relatives

Snakes are **Reptiles**. There are more than 2,300 kinds of snakes. They all hunt other animals for food. Most snakes live in warm parts of the world.

crowned snake

royal python

green mamba

diamondback
rattlesnake

Some snakes are **venomous.** Others are
harmless. Rattlesnakes are venomous
snakes. This book is about rattlesnakes.

5

What Rattlesnakes Look Like

Snakes have long bodies. They do not have legs. Their bodies are covered with tiny **scales**. Scales are hard and dry. Look closely. See how the scales all face one way?

Snakes come in many colors. Many snake skins have patterns. Colors and patterns help snakes to hide. This diamondback rattlesnake **blends** in with the stones.

Where Rattlesnakes Live

There are thirty-one kinds of rattlesnakes. They live in parts of North and South America. Diamondback rattlesnakes live in this desert.

In the fall, the desert gets cold. Rattlesnakes begin to eat more food. They are getting ready to **hibernate.** When it is time, they go into a hole and sleep through the winter.

Moving

The desert is cold at night. In the morning, rattlesnakes find a sunny spot. They get warm by **basking** in the sun. To cool off, they move to a shady spot.

Snakes move forward by pushing against something. This snake pushes the **scales** on its belly against rocks. Then the snake pulls itself up and over them. Snakes can slide, glide, and climb

Finding Food

This rattlesnake is hungry. How will she find food? She uses her **forked** tongue to smell a wood rat. Two **pits** under her eyes help her to feel the heat of the rat's body.

The snake cannot hear the rat. She has no ears. She uses her tongue, pits, and eyes to find it. She can now see the rat. She winds her body into a coil. She is ready to **strike.**

Eating

A rattlesnake has two hollow teeth called fangs. When the rattlesnake bites the wood rat, **venom** flows out of the fangs. The poison kills the rat.

The rattlesnake opens her mouth wide. Her **scales** and ribs stretch so the rat can fit inside her. She eats the rat whole. Snakes also eat rabbits, lizards, frogs, and eggs.

Babies

Many snakes lay eggs. Rattlesnakes give birth to live babies. They have from two to twenty-five babies at the end of summer. This baby rattlesnake is just being born.

A baby snake may not be the same color as its mother. The pattern of its **scales** may be different, too. As it grows, its scales change. One day, the baby will look like its mother.

Growing Up

Mother snakes do not take care of their babies. Babies take care of themselves. Babies know how to find food. They know how to get warm. They even know how to bite.

Baby snakes shed their skin because they
grow out of it. Old skin peels off when
new skin is ready. The skin at the nose
peels first.

Danger

A rattlesnake has a rattle at the end of its tail. The rattle grows each time the snake sheds its skin. The snake lifts its tail and shakes the rattle. The rattle makes a *buzzing* sound. This sound tells animals to stay away.

Some people hunt rattlesnakes for their skins. Skins are used to make belts and purses. People must be careful. Rattlesnakes will bite a person who comes too close.

Rattlesnake Facts

- Male and female rattlesnakes look the same, but males are bigger.

- Male diamondbacks can grow to 7 feet (2 m) long.

- Adults shed their skins when it gets worn out. Rattlesnakes shed their skin about 2 or 3 times a year.

- Rattlesnakes can live for many months without food. If they can't find food, they can live off the fat stored in their bodies.

- Rattlesnakes are good swimmers. They will swim to find food or a **mate**.

Glossary

basking warming up in the sun

blends mixes together with something

forked to be divided but not separate, like the letter *V*

hibernate to sleep through the winter

mate to find a partner to have babies with

pits holes

reptile animals with hard, dry scales that must bask in the sun to keep their body temperatures warm

scales hard skin that covers the bodies of reptiles

strike to hit or attack

venom poison

venomous something that has poison

Index

More Books To Read

Arnosky, Jim. *All About Rattlesnakes*. New York: Scholastic, Incorporated, 1997.

Robinson, Fay. *Great Snakes!* New York: Scholastic, Incorporated, 1996.